Animals with HANGOVERS

St. Martin's Griffin
NEW YORK

Animals with
HANGOVERS

THE MORNING AFTER IS NEVER CUTE

Dave Johnston

No animals were forced to consume alcoholic beverages in the making of this book.

Library of Congress Cataloging-in-Publication Data is on file.

Manufactured in China

Animals with Hangovers is produced by becker&mayer!, Bellevue, Washington.
www.beckermayer.com

For information, address
St. Martin's Press, 175 Fifth Avenue, New York, N.Y. 10010
www.stmartins.com

Design by Rosebud Eustace
Editorial by Amy Wideman
Photo research by Jessica Eskelsen and Amelia Boldaji
Production coordination by Leah Finger

ISBN 978-0-312-64168-9

First Edition: October 2011

10 9 8 7 6 5 4 3 2 1

Dedication

This book is dedicated to every animal who has been taunted by repeated tennis ball fake-outs, made to roll over, mocked by unattainable laser-pointer lights, forced to wear a Halloween costume, or endlessly hounded to say, "Rye ruv roo."

Believe me, we wouldn't do it if you weren't so damned adorable.

After getting home
from the bar, Howard
spent the rest of the
evening transfixed by
the ceiling fan.

"Did I drink crème de menthe last night, or did I eat the toothpaste?"

"I feel like Lady Macbeth, except for me, it's the stench of gin I can't wash away."

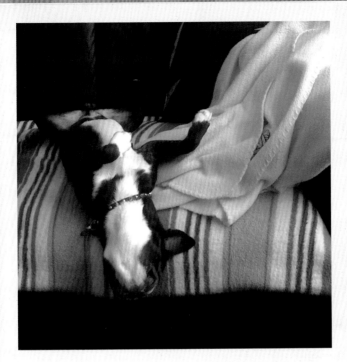

"Ohh, it's like there's a slide show of shame running through my brain. Why did you let me do karaoke?!"

"Be a peach and go get a bottle of Mommy's medicine. Yes, that's right, the clear one in the freezer with the eagle on it. And bring some olives, too."

It was soon apparent to Celeste that leaving the house in the daylight had been a terrible, terrible mistake.

Lonnie's mom had told him to have no regrets in life. Though if she'd seen him the previous evening, she might have given him different advice.

"Dear Lord, if you cure this hangover, I swear I will go to church for the rest of my life. If not, I will eat a Bible. Ball's in your court. Amen."

Knowing her post-party track record,
Nicole's friends made sure the bucket
was safely inside the "splash zone."

Despite what he told friends after a couple of beers, Earl could not still fit into his high school basketball uniform. Not unless it was being used as a tourniquet.

It was not the first time Katrina had passed out on the toilet. It was, however, the first time she did it on one that had been left for trash pickup.

"I woke up in a compost pile with a banana peel stuck to my forehead. How do you think I feel?"

19

Lucy's coworkers were starting to suspect that she enjoyed her coffee way too much for it to actually be coffee.

"Oh my God, where are my car keys?
Where is my car?
Where is my dignity?"

Trish intended to get up just as soon as she figured out which way "up" was.

"I've had a few truly great regrets in my life,
and they all stem from last night."

"The worst part about making out with the cab driver is that he kept the meter running the entire time."

25

"How do I feel? Like an astronaut dropped a bowling ball on my head from orbit. Other than that, absolutely terrible."

"I think it's best if we give Donny a little space. It's only a matter of time before he turns from a melancholy drunk into a punch-anything-that-moves drunk."

If he hadn't already objected twice during the ceremony, the father of the bride would have made his feelings quite clear when he passed out during the best man's toast.

"One too many?
If one now equals
seven, then yes."

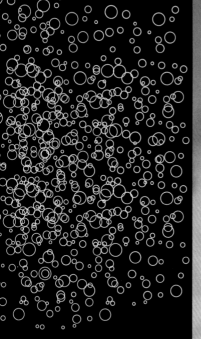

Kelly's friends said they'd seen worse exits from a bar, but the road rash on her forehead told a very different story.

The relationship was never the same after
Paul threw up on Bunny's lap.

"What has four thumbs and needs someone to call the fire department?"

"Bleckk . . . shame tastes almost exactly like tequila."

As she slipped off to sleep, Dorothy felt
a momentary twinge of regret at making
out with "Conjunctivitis Carl."

"What does an older guy like me have to offer?
Do you mean besides a ton of life experience and
the guts to wear a blue terry cloth poncho?"

Waking up with somebody else's foot in her mouth, Beverly decided that would be the last time she ever said, "Feel free to crash at my place."

39

Bella disagreed with her mother's advice, as "a little color" had done nothing to improve her mood, much less her hangover.

Glen felt that what set him apart was his take-no-prisoners attitude and his knowledge of bar trivia. The other patrons agreed it was his ill-fitting toupee.

Needless to say, everybody at the tennis club was quite aware of Duff's drinking problem.

"Believe me, I already tried putting cucumber
slices over my eyes."

"I don't see why it's a big deal. Lots of people have a bottle of wine with dinner."

"Thanks so much for waking me. You realize, of course, that if I could lift any part of my body, I'd kill you."

Brianna felt refreshed as she awoke surrounded by the natural splendor of the sun-dappled grass. That feeling vanished when her neighbor's sprinklers turned on.

One sip of beer and suddenly the memory of making out with the parking lot attendant came rushing back to Louise. Worse, she still had to go pick up her car.

Whenever parents wanted to warn their
children about the dangers of drinking,
they just pointed at Danny.

Eventually, James and Jamal would learn that "the ladies" were, in fact, quite resistant to the "pouty face."

Diane realized two things simultaneously: she had a drinking problem, and she needed to reorganize her shoes.

Nancy's head, weighed down by a night of
tequila blasters and McPherson's all-morning
talk about fiscal restraint in regard to the
usage of coffee filters, slowly sank to the
surface of the conference room table.

"The one word that explains how I'm feeling right now is 'fragile.'"

"Your mother and I have been waiting up all night for you."

"Is that alcohol on your breath? More importantly, are you wearing the welcome mat?"

Pablo was confident nobody at the office would know he was still drunk from the night before. As usual, Pablo's confidence was misplaced.

"I don't think I can take another step. Remember me at brunch."

In the light of day they all agreed that the most problematic part of threesomes was positioning.

"You damn kids don't know how good you have it. When I was your age, we had to make our own alcohol out of rocks and twigs. Also, I had to walk 15 miles to school carrying a herring."

61

Kate sat in the bathtub and wondered where her night had gone wrong. Of course, the obvious answer was the moment she walked through the bar's plate glass door.

Judith was having a great time at her bachelorette party until she realized that the police officer/male stripper was her Uncle Jimmy.

"On a scale of 1 to 10, I would say that I'm very, very intoxicated."

"So, a monkey walks into a bar . . ."

Despite a promise he'd made to himself before the Christmas party, Linus woke up wearing an elf costume for the second year in a row.

Regaining consciousness on the bar floor, Jo considered how many embarrassing moments in her life had been preceded by the words, "Watch this!"

"So, you know how they say 'beer before liquor, never sicker'? Somebody should have said, 'sangria before White Russians, call Poison Control immediately.'"

Friends had learned to avoid Paulina when she put her "drink'n sweater" on. Also, whenever she replaced "ing" with "'n."

Uncle Mikey was known for three things: his charity work, his love of classic cars, and his complete inability to follow social norms when he drank.

"Whoever suggested tequila shots is a dead man."

"I'm trying not to panic, but it feels like someone knitted a tiny sweater around my tongue."

"OK, fine, I had one too many.
Will you get off my back?"

Francisco, Kenny, and Tyler swore to never speak of that night again.

Ken wore his black eyes
as a badge of honor,
though they were just
evidence he had walked
into a parking meter.

"Honestly, after what happened, I
don't know if you're the right person
to be calling me a jackass."

The next day, Sergei would blame his stiffness on sleeping weird. He made no mention of the banana daiquiris.

When Damon asked if anybody wanted a cognac, there was something in his stare that made them all decline.

It would be another ten minutes before it dawned on Terrance that he was flirting with a tree.

On the occasions he did find a message in a bottle, Silas was terribly disappointed at the meaningless waste of a bottle.

"If you must know, I'm refusing to acknowledge the existence of morning."

"I realize now that I shouldn't have ordered that third pitcher of beer. Also, I should never drink alone."

"I was wrong. Breakfast isn't going to cure this hangover. Let's try lunch."

The note he found on the nightstand thanked "Kevin" for the great time. Obviously, Timmy had made quite the impression on her.

"Sleeping on the floor is good for my back. Losing consciousness on it was just a happy coincidence."

"Whoa there, cowboy, what do you mean
you've already announced last call?"

Drinking changed Megan.

"I truly believe that if I took these off, the amount of alcohol in my bloodstream would cause my eyeballs to burst into flame. Let's not take any unnecessary chances."

"Hey, three hours late for my party and you're the first one here. Let me get you a hat."

Awash in shame, Maurice knew his days of barhopping were over.

Kitty often said there was nothing like "an adventure in the great outdoors," though it might have been more accurate if she'd said "drinking a 40-ouncer on the sidewalk."

Sadly for Lewis, the one word most commonly used to describe him was "overserved."

"Unless a group of ninjas snuck into my bedroom last night and beat me with plastic baseball bats, I have no reasonable explanation for why I feel this bad."

"How about a little sugar?"

The first thing that Lisa lost when she was drinking was her sense of decorum, followed shortly by the ability to control the volume level of her own voice.

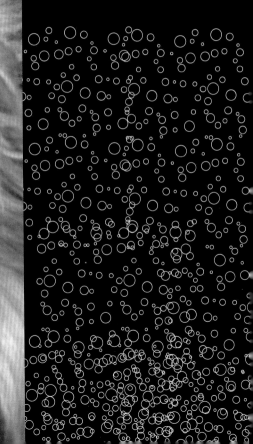

Everybody thought Vance
was the life of the party. His
girlfriend Clarice, however,
was the death of it.

"After what happened last night with Arthur, I can't help but feel a little dirty."

"Sweetie pie, do you remember us doing anything last night that would explain the SWAT team in the front yard?"

"All I ask is that you don't judge me. Or at least wait until I leave the room."

"Can't a guy lying in the bushes by the side of the road get a little privacy?"

The ladies thought Jack was flirting, but he was just trying to make out the happy hour specials.

"Your mockery cannot possibly make me feel any worse than I already do. Now, if you would kindly carry me inside."

"Hey neighbor, have a little too much vino last night?"

No matter how cool he tried to play it, Frank always came off as desperately horny.

Sometimes when he drank, Larry would sit and contemplate the enormity of the universe. Mostly, he would just stare at women doing yoga.

It was the last time Corey ever suggested drunken trust falls.

"As God is my witness, I swear I will never drink again."

Dimitri, unfortunately, was unable to figure out the connection between a long night of drinking with the boys, no eye drops, and another failed job interview.

The fetal position hadn't worked for
Bob since he was very, very young.

Like opening presents early and oyster stuffing, Aunt Erma's annual eggnog binge was a holiday tradition.

Somewhere out there in the world, Darryl knew
there was a bar that had his credit card. He hoped
they might be able to tell him where his shoes went.

"Apparently she's not drinking anymore."

A few glasses of wine made Ava lose her inhibitions. A few more made her lose her cell phone in the toilet.

Of all the places Margaret had woken up, the
middle of a field really wasn't that bad.

Tamara dreamed of getting a new job, which was oddly prophetic because she would need one after falling asleep during her performance review.

"Not everybody can shotgun eight beers, so I thought, 'Why not put that on my résumé?'"

127

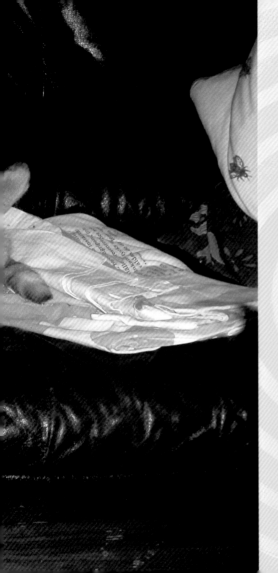

After a lengthy internal debate, Cathy decided the only way she was going to get over her hangover was to smoke a lot more pot.

Kyle's "come hither" look was really more of a "run for your life" look.

"I don't want to open my eyes, because I'm afraid of what this hangover looks like in the mirror."

Occasionally when she was drunk, Olive would attempt to make her boyfriend's brain explode using her thoughts.

Velma's night had gone to hell in a handbasket.

It was too late. Simon had already seen the "Doubles for $1 More!" sign.

"Could my night have gone worse?
Sure, I guess I could have accidentally
tasered my future father-in-law *twice*."

Daniel couldn't believe that, once again, Kelly had gotten him into bed with a mixture of sweet talk and light beer.

"A horse walks into a bar. The bartender says, 'Why the long face?'"

Debbie slept soundly, knowing that her hangover would still be there when she woke up.

It was hard for bartenders to say no to Steve, mostly because it seemed he was incapable of understanding the word.

Trish complained about never having anything clean to wear, but she never mentioned that she regularly passed out in the laundry pile.

142

Brian realized that nothing is worse than sobering up during a one-night stand.

143

"Hello, I was wondering if you found a wallet in your cab last night . . . Yes, it would still be inside a pair of pants . . . No, I have no idea why I took off my pants, either."

"I keep running last night through my head and I can't stop thinking I should have left the pole dancing to the professionals."

Willie was not one for moderation. This was especially true for cocktails that tasted like fruit punch.

Scott always ate his way out of hangovers. He had a *lot* of hangovers.

148

149

Joey loved his new haircut,
though it caused him to
fall down the bar's
staircase twice.

Mavis and Charles realized at the exact same moment that they had no idea what the other's name was.

Jessica knew she couldn't hide from her problems for the rest of her life, but she'd settle for the rest of the day.

"Like my mother always said, 'feed a cold, starve a fever, and wrap a hangover in a duvet and let it lie down on the couch.'"

Dwayne had learned from experience that when he was drunk enough to see multiple copies of his girlfriend, it was best to listen only to the one in the middle.

"Why don't we turn that light back off, 'kay?"

"No, really, I can't tell you how much I appreciate a surprise fortieth birthday party. And yay, I see that my stepbrother Clay is here. Who gave him my address?"

157

As always, George stayed true to his personal motto: Only drink on days of the week with "y" in them.

Darla screamed when she woke up because she thought there was an animal in her bed. Luckily, it was just one of her hair extensions.

As she came to, Jasmine accepted that she should have known better than to pass out on crafts night.

"I wanted a hat that says, 'Hola, I'm Señor Fun Times!' but I feel like it says, 'Hello, I Have An Inordinately Large Head.'"

"If I were to tell you this is the highlight of my night, would you believe me?"

163

"Let's not tell anybody at the office about this. Agreed?"

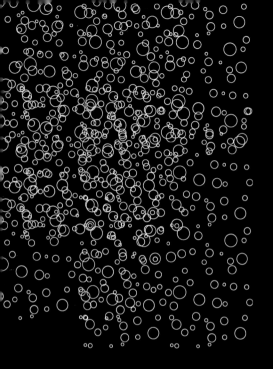

The next morning
Scott would assume
that someone had
broken into his house
and scattered fast food
wrappers in his bed.

Quality You Can Taste®
Since 1948.

IN·N·OUT®
BURGER

Sadly, Donna was woefully unprepared for an entire evening of "getting lei'd" jokes.

Despite Sam's vivid imagination, his "superpowers" included neither flight nor the ability to handle his liquor well.

"'Ello, is your father a thief? No? Zen who stole the stars and put zem in your eyes?"

Eric suddenly remembered that his "friends" had convinced him to run naked down the street. It would be another hour before he discovered they'd painted him pink.

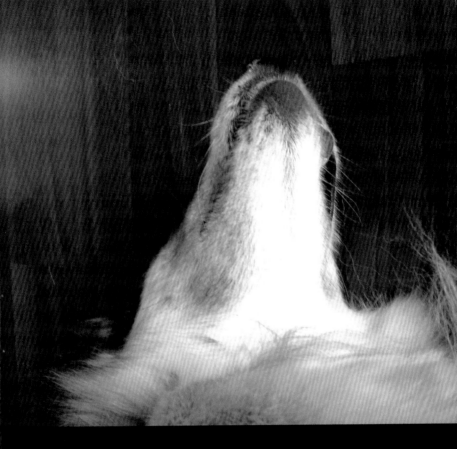

Since he was a terrible tipper, the bartenders rarely checked to see if Charlie was still breathing.

Kyle learned that everybody loves the "crazy party guy" until they're blinded by the glare of an unshaded lamp the instant before being hit in the eye with a champagne cork.

Montgomery smelled the winds of change,
which meant his clothes were probably
finished drying.

Andrea would spend an hour trying to get the glass to slide closer using telekinesis.

Marcus saved time by combining his hangovers with panic attacks.

"Sorry, I didn't mean to bite your head off, buddy. I just had a bad night."

Gregor would rue the day he stumbled out of a bar and into the path of a high school cross-country team.

Dolly would later question her initial delight at the prospect of grape-flavored vodka.

"I can think of only two cures for this miserable hangover. How about you give me a tummy rub and I won't subject you to the second one."

It was a beautiful view, but Travis had no idea how he got on the neighbor's roof.

"Am I still drunk? Is a bear in the woods Catholic?"

"Darling, if I don't get a Bloody Mary in the
next five minutes, I swear I'm going to stab
our waitress."

There are times in a person's life when they just want to crawl into the liquor cabinet. Gary took that a step further.

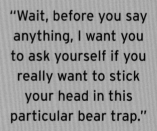

"Wait, before you say anything, I want you to ask yourself if you really want to stick your head in this particular bear trap."

After a night of drinking Long Island iced teas, Leslie felt it was healthy to elevate her liver. Interestingly, Leslie had never considered not drinking Long Island iced teas for her health.

Despite her best efforts and a naturally low center of gravity, it would be hours before Danielle's world stopped spinning.

"Well, you don't have to go home, but you certainly can't stay here."

While Luna was just terribly hungover when she had her passport photo taken, airport security tended to interpret her expression as "sinister mastermind."

Another marriage needlessly impacted by the potent combination of a couple glasses of wine and a game of backgammon.

If one could rate a party by the number of guests still lying on the floor the next day, theirs was truly a success.

Gabriel paled at the idea of Tequila Tuesday.
Especially with the memory of Malt Liquor Monday
and Sangria Sunday so fresh in his mind.

Hazel's life had been one long series of bad decisions all leading to last night's wet T-shirt contest.

Jill always came off as a little judgmental.

"There's no reason to panic, Maria. I'm sure you can figure out where you are. Wait, is that sign in Cyrillic? OK, time to panic."

Right before he woke up with a pounding headache, Yoon had a very pleasant dream about a free all-you-can-eat salad bar.

Acknowledgments

I owe immeasurable gratitude, chest scratches, and love to Thalia, Sophie, and Maeb. Also, I would be remiss if I didn't mention the important contributions and friendship of Hook Mahone, Jackson, Callahan, Hextall, Doc, Gilbert, Dewey, Hattie, and Mr. Ping Pong. My special thanks go to the Comet, Barça, Bimbo's, and the Cha Cha for their assistance with fact-finding for this book, as well as my research associates for their assistance with the tireless pursuit of truth.

About the Author

Dave Johnston is a writer whose work has appeared on McSweeneys.net, as well as in *The McSweeney's Joke Book of Book Jokes* (2008), and he is the author of *Make the Bible Work for You* (2008) and *Dear Mr. Johnston* (2008). His writing can also be found at schmeattle.blogspot.com. As a longtime Seattle bartender, he is intimately familiar with every variation of the hangover.

Image Credits

Every effort has been made to trace copyright holders. If any unintended omissions have been made, becker&mayer! would be pleased to add appropriate acknowledgments in future editions. Photos from flickr.com used under Creative Commons license: http://creativecommons.org/licenses/by/2.0